Paganism Explained

Part V:
Ásgarðr, Vanaheimr & the Nine Worlds of Hel

By Varg Vikernes & Marie Cachet

Table of Contents

Rune Lore

We tend to differentiate between myths and fairy tales, as if they are two completely different things altogether. The myths deal with the gods and their world in a poetic language, and the fairy tales seem to deal with ordinary people and their world with prose. As we have showed you before, in 'Paganism Explained' part 2 and 3, they contain the excact same riddles and secrets.

The myths explain reincarnation from a religious perspective, whilst the fairy tales explain the same from an older traditional perspective. The myths are younger than the fairy tales and came with religion (which in term came with agriculture, in the Neolithics).

As explained in 'Sorcery and Religion in Ancient Scandinavia' the animist tradition co-existed with the religious tradition. The latter never replaced the former. More than anything, the religion just supplemented the old tradition. It was still the same, only with some things changed, like anthropomorphised spirits. Then when Christianity arrived, a *religion* from the Hebrew desert, it crashed and clashed first and foremost with the Pagan *religion*, because this was it's direct competitor, and not as much with the older Pagan tradition.

Because of that, the fairy tales managed to better fly under the Christian radar, so to speak, and survived to a much larger extent than the myths did.

We still have both myths and fairy tales, and even though they are slightly different from each other in format and style, we recognize the same patterns in them, and can tell that they tell the same story and in essence are the same. Together they make up our mythology. Our Rune Lore.

Reincarnation

As we have already showed you in this series of booklets, our myths and fairy tales tend to deal with one single topic: reincarnation. They describe it with much the same metaphors, but this way or that way, with focus on this or that. But they describe the same; the reincarnation.

The question then arrises: "Why so many myths about the same?"

The purpose of the myth was to give the child an opportunity to understand it. If he did not, he would later on be told another myth, and then another myth, etc., until he would be able to see the pattern, and when he did, he would understand them all at once.

In order to do so, in order to achieve this, they made many myths about the same, many fairy tales about the same.

Therefore, when we explain these myths and fairy tales today, we repeat ourselves. We end up telling you about reincarnation, over and over again. Because that is the purpose of the Rune Lore (myths and the fairy tales); to tell you about reincarnation, its purpose, its function, its meaning. Its *significance* to us all.

The Sacred

You can treat amnesia in a patient today by showing him items that meant something to him before the amnesia, by having people he cared about talk to him and by bringing him to locations that he was emotionally connected to somehow. Likewise, you can enter the burial mound of your forebears and see the items they were buried with, touch and feel them, you can expose yourself to situations that your forebears were in and you can go to places where they lived or that were important to them emotionally.

Therefore we have sacred object, like Yule trees and Yule decorations. Therefore we have high festivals and rituals. Therefore we have temples. To lift the amnesia of death.

Therefore we have all these myths and fairy tales about reincarnation. They are instructions on how to reincarnate.

Divine Power

Many think reincarnation gives you the ability to literally remember previous lives. Your name, profession, events, loved ones, address, cause of death etc., and tend to ask the question: "Who were you in your previous life?"

Now, I don't rule out concrete memories from previous lives, but I don't think this is the purpose of reincarnation or the purpose of learning about it.

You don't even remember everything from your own life. Not from your childhood, not from last year, not from a week ago, not from yesterday, and some times in relation to some things not even from earlier the same day. Memory has a purpose, and although we don't actually understand everything surrounding this today, we must relate to the fact that we don't remember everything. We easily and often fast slip into forgetfulness. Only a reminder will bring back the forgotten memories.

But what if you in an instant remembered all the joys and victories of your life; would it not lift your spirit if you did? There and then, light up and banish all darkness and shadows from your mind?

If you *lived with* this uplifting sensation permanently burnt into your mind and marrow, would it not make you a braver, saner, kinder, safer and in short a *better* person?

...and there you have it: the *purpose* of reincarnation and of spending so much time and energy on it.

The sum of all these joys and victories of all your forebears, every single one of them contributing to it more or less, is what our forebears called *Hamingja* ("walking in shapes"). This is what walks in shapes, follows your kin through the ages and gives you good luck in life.

But is luck even real?

The Norwegian term for luck: *hell* means "whole", "healthy", "unharmed", but derives from Norse *heill*, proto-Nordic **hailagaR*, from PIE **kolio*, from the root **kel-*, meaning "to conceal", "to cover".

Perhaps interestingly, it derives from the same PIE root as the -höll in Valhöll derives from, the same as the deity name Hel derives from.

You could say that luck covers and conceals you from the darkness of this world, and keeps you whole, in good health and unharmed.

In Roman mythology luck is personified in Fortuna, the godddess of good fortune. Her festival was on Midsummer Day, and she corresponds to our Freyja.

But is luck real? I think so yes. I can probably not prove it, but experience tells me that I am right. I leave it you to decide whether or not you believe in it too.

In relation to our Rune Lore whether or not we believe luck is real is not relevant: Those who made the myths and fairy tales did believe it was real, so we need to read/hear the myths with that in mind.

About Patterns in our Rune Lore

When the Christians in Scandinavia first started to talk about our myths, in the 19th century, they tried to either belittle the Native European myths, or they tried to Christianize them. They were taught that for a mythology to be worth anything it needed to contain a creation, an armageddon and of course morality. So even though none of this existed in the Scandinavian mythology, they tried to find it and interpreted everything in light of this. Or rather, in this pitch black darkness...

Fumbling about in this Judeo-Christian shadow, they failed to see the real meaning.

What we can tell from our Rune Lore, from our myths and fairy tales, is that not only is there no 'morality' in them, but the lack of morality is used as a means for an end. The children were, as I have already told you, meant to *understand* these runes. When they did not, they were told more fairy tales or more myths. Again: because they were meant to understand them. They would if they discovered a *pattern*.

Let me give you an example.

E. g. the protagonist in the Scandinavian fairy tale about Askeladden who enters an eating contest with a troll. He initially enters the forest of a troll to cut wood and is caught stealing. Yes, he trespasses on somebody else's property in order to steal from him. When caught he tricks the troll into stabbing itself to death, by cutting its own stomach open. He then proceeds to steal all the troll's gold and silver – and leaves the rightful owner of both the forest and the precious metals to bleed to death in his own home.

The protagonist is *not* acting according to normally accepted behaviour. This is a *pattern* found in all our myths and fairy tales.

So when you understand this, you *will* realize that the myth or fairy tale *has another meaning and purpose*. And *that* is a means used to help the child find that real meaning and purpose.

Morals are not found in mythology, but in our Native European *instincts*. You don't need to learn it, and if you fail to behave morally, Mother Nature effectively removed you from procreation. Also, the tribe would react more directly to your immorality, first with banishment for some time, usually a year and a day, and then if you still failed to behave (after you returned home), they would remove you permanently.

Another means used for the same purpose is the use of *impossabilities*. What described in the myths and fairy tales *is impossible in real life*. A female troll carrying her head under her arm? Eight legged horses that can fly through the air? Gods that change into birds or flies? Wagons pulled by goats flying through the air? Come on! Anyone with the most basic understanding of reality, even a child, can tell that this is impossible!

No, they did not believe in these things in the past. They knew perfectly well that this was impossible.

...and when you know that, you can find the *real* meaning instead. Basic deduction. You strip all other possabilities, you end up with only one possible solution. You have to find it, in the end.

If you still don't find it after all those chances and all that help?

Vituð ér enn, eða hvat? ("Do you still don't know enough [to find the meaning] or what?"

Sigh.

Ásgarðr

Before we start talking about Ásgarðr and the other divine realms I will ask you to unlearn everything you thought you knew about this topic. Ignore it all. Whatever you heard or read in a book or online, forget it. Instead assume that you know nothing and then we together will look at what the original sources actually say. Not what Christian scholars claim the sources tell us, but straight forward: what do they *actually* and *in themselves* tell us?

If you continue reading assuming you already know what Ásgarðr is, you will probably not be able to learn much. To fill your head with the truth, it cannot be half-filled with lies already. Pour out the lies first.

Ignorance is not the worst. The worst is to think you know when you don't. So let us start from scratch.

We will start with the Norse and the Etymological dictionary, to find out what Ásgarðr is.

The term áss (plural æsir, feminine ásynja) is normally understood as a Norse term for 'god'. But the term derives from younger proto-Nordic ans, from older proto-Nordic ansuR, from proto-Germanic ansuz, from the proto-Indo-European root *ans-/*and-, meaning simply 'breath'. So it doesn't actually mean 'god'. It means 'breath', just like the Latin term spiritus does. We are just told by the scholars that it means 'god', because the Æsir are understood as 'gods'.

Garðr means 'yard', 'farm' or 'world/home'.

So although we have it presented to us as "the world of the gods", it actually means "the world of those with a breath". And who has a breath? Yes, the living. It is not some fancy world in the sky, but the world of the living. Ásgarðr is our world, that we live and breathe in.

We learn from Hymiskviða that:

7.
Fóru drjúgum
dag þann fram
Ásgarði frá,
unz til Egils kvámu;
hirði hann hafra
horngöfgasta;
hurfu at höllu,
er Hymir átti.

7.
Far they travelled
that day
from Ásgarðr
to Egill they came.
He housed he-goats
with beautiful horns;
they went
to Hymir's hall.

What this says is not that the gods travelled somewhere in space or from some divine realm, but that they... died. They left the world of the living (those with a breath), so they pretty much had to die. No breath, no human life. Simple. When we know what Ásgarðr really is, it cannot be misunderstood... in theory.

Hymir is also known as Ægir ('sea') and in mythology 'the sea' is always a metaphor for the amniotic fluid. You don't believe me? Ok. You will see later that I am right.

Hymir is a word game with Ymir, which means "the twin", and as explained in 'Paganism Explained Part III' and in 'The Secret of the She-Bear', the twin is the placenta-ancestor. The giant/dragon that has to be slain, when you are born; you cut its neck, the umbilical cord, and the placenta dies. The monster's head is cut off.

The he-goats with golden horns are mentioned because they are instrumental to the quest. The Æsir are there to get a new cauldron for themselves. A new womb that can bring them back to live. They travel to

Hymir because he has such a cauldron, but also the very important he-goats with golden horns in his hall. The he-goats are the absolutely necessary adrenaline, Cernunnos/Loki/Pan, as talked about in 'Paganism Explained Part III'.

The other myths where Ásgarðr is (briefly) mentioned talk about Ásgarðr in the same sense: it's a place the Æsir travel to (from Hel or Jötunnheimr) or from (to go to Hel or Jötunnheimr).

So Ásgarðr is *not* some "Heavenly realm" in the sky, as proposed by the Christian scholars. It is our own world; the world of those with a breath.

As for the divine homes found inside Ásgarðr, Valhöll is thoroughly described in Paganism Explained IV. What the other homes are were explained in the book 'Sorcery and Religion in Ancient Scandinavia' and will be briefly repeated later in this booklet.

Vanaheimr

Then you have that other world of deities mentioned in the Scandinavian mythology, Vanaheimr, where – according to modern scholars – another race of gods lived; the Vanir.

The Vanir are the twins Freyr and Freyja, and their father Njörðr.

But let us first dissect the term Vanaheimr. *Vanir* is a plural form of masculine *vanr*, meaning 'water'. The feminine form of the term is *dís* (pluralis *dísir*), meaning 'woman'. The latter is also related to the term *dýs*, meaning 'small burial mound'.

Heimr means simply 'home'. So Vanaheimr is 'the home of water', related to women and 'small burial mounds'. Ok.

With all of that in mind, one can easily think of water as amniotic fluid, found in women, when they are pregnant and have a belly looking like a small burial mound. Let us wait a bit with that though.

What about the Vanir/Dísir living there? Who and what are they?

Let us take Freyja first. A deity linked to the Moon and the burial mound, the most beautiful of all the goddesses and the one all the ettins want. Her name means 'seed', and the Moon is an obvious metaphor for eggs. So that's real easy: Freyja is the egg in the woman.

The ettins trying to kidnap her is the endometrium, a carpet of crystallized blood, catching the egg in the womb of the woman. They are 'frost ettins' because the blood is crystallized. If the egg is not fertilized they catch and wash the egg out from the womb of the woman – in form of fire ettins ([not crystallized] menstrual blood).

….and yes, this is Jötunnheimr ('home of the ettins'). One of the places the deities travel to or from.

Her twin brother is Freyr, whose name also means 'seed', and yes, this is the spermatozoid fertilizing the egg. We have it explained rather clearly in Skírnismál where Freyr sends his servant, Skírnir ('shining one'), equipped with Freyr's sword (his manhood), down to Gerð ('belt', 'equipment'), to propose to her from him. We here see Freyja as Gerð, and yes, she is found in the 'belt' area of the woman. She rejects him, but finally accepts when threatened with a magic wand. If she does not accept, she will be washed out with the menstrual blood, by the ettins – as an unfertilized egg.

When Gerð accepts Freyr, he still has to wait for her to marry him for a few days. Perhaps because it takes some time for the spermatozoid to attach itself to the egg.

Their father, Njörðr, is the deity of the fertile sea, the amniotic fluid, where the fertilized egg grows into a human being. His ship is the placenta, that they ride in the 'sea'.

So whilst Ásgarðr is the world of the living, Vanaheimr is the womb of the woman, when she is pregnant.

The Æsir-Vanir War

Now that we understand that Ásgarðr is the world of the living and Vanaheimr is the womb of the woman, then how can we explain the mythic war between the Æsir and the Vanir?

What we have commonly learnt, from scholars, is that this describes a meeting of different races of gods, and that they entered a multicultural mode and ended up in a harmonious race-mixed society. Or we have learnt that this describes how a feminine fertility cult in the Germanic area was invaded by a more aggressive and manly warrior cult, and of that this is supported by the Indo-European invasion hypothesis. Or the other way around, that this supports this hypothesis.

The first of these hypotheses is just a wild speculation intended to support (and motivated by) modern anti-European lie-propaganda. There is no evidence whatsoever to support this hypothesis. On the contrary; we see a continuous tradition in the Germanic area from the Stone Age.

The same fact disproves the Indo-European hypothesis, as this too suggests that some sort of different cult came to the Germanic area and either replaced their tradition or at least dramatically changed it. No such replacement or change has occurred. The only change we see is that I already spoke of above with the introduction of agriculture, in the Neolithic Age, several thousand years before any Indo-Europeans arrived in Scandinavia (according to scholars). Even in the Neolithic Age nothing was really changed, save the anthropomorphising of spirits. This was only an addition, and a continuation of the same.

So the Indo-European hypothesis too is simply not true.

Further, I am rather surprised by the lack of reasoning in the scholars who propose this, as the war between the Æsir and Vanir ends in a tie, because none of them are strong enough to win. Why would a manly warrior cult not be strong enough to win over a feminine fertility cult?! Knowing that the Æsir are numerically vastly superior to the Vanir makes this even more absurd. This makes no sense.

Their motivation for claiming this has nothing to do with the evidence provided to them. This is just what some of them *want* to be true, because they need support for their horribly lacking "Indo-European invasion" hypothesis.

So I will adamantly claim that both the above mentioned hypothesis are wrong and disproven.

Then we move on to the next stage, and where we can explain what the Æsir-Vanir war was all about.

Let me first remind you about what happened in that war:

Óðinn led an army of Æsir to attack the Vanir, and initiated the battle by casting his spear upon the enemies, but the Vanir were well prepared for an attack. None of them achieved victory, so they agreed to establish a truce and exchange hostages. The Vanir sent the wealthy Njörðr to the Æsir, and the Æsir sent the large and handsome Hønir and the wise Mímir to the Vanir.

The Vanir made Hønir their chieftain, but unless Mímir was there with him, he was rather useless, and only said; "let somebody else decide." The Vanir felt cheated. They seized Mímir, cut his head off and sent it to Ásgarðr. Óðinn took Mímir's head, embalmed it with herbs and cast spells on it, which gave it the power to speak and tell him secrets.

He then declared the Vanir gods, just like the Æsir.

The 'battle' started when Óðinn threw his spear. From 'Paganism Explained Part IV' you could learn that his spear is a metaphor for the umbilical cord. There is no 'war' in other words. It's just an army of spermatozoids entering Vanaheimr, fertilizing an egg. Thus the 'spear' is attached. When the egg is fertilized, naturally a sea of amniotic fluid (Njörðr) is created by the mother, and the baby (Hønir) and it's twin, the placenta (Mímir), enter Vanaheimr.

Before we continue, let us examine the names, and also remember that Hønir and Mímir are also known as Víli and Véi respectively, the brothers of Óðinn.

Hønir means "give sign".
Vílir means "will".

Mímir means "reminiscence".
Véi means "sacred".

The rather simple-minded baby does indeed 'give sign' when it wills, when it is ready to be born; it knocks it's head on the cervix of the mother, to signal that it is ready to be born. There is little more to say about that.

But the case of Mímir is much more complex. Let me explain.

As said before, in this series, and as explained in 'The Secret of the She-Bear', the placenta is the sum of the forebears, or rather *all* the forebears at once. It transfers memories ('reminiscence') of previous lives via the umbilical cord, the well of Mímir, to the fetus, to Hønir. It educates the child even before it is born. When the Vanir cuts his head off, it means simply that the child is born, and naturally the umbilical cord is cut. The head of Mímir too is sent back to Ásgarðr, the world of the living.

Interestingly though, Óðinn preserves this sacred head, the placenta, *to learn from it*. And yes, you can learn a lot from studying the placenta. Unfortunately this is an art that was lost to us, during and after the Renaissance, when the Judeo-Christians persecuted and murdered our midwives (whom they called "witches").

The midwives, known from mythology as the Norns, studied the placenta, and could tell from it's shape, size and other properties about the *fate* of the person it had 'educated' in a womb. Funnily enough, modern science has begun to re-discover this lost art, and recognizes today that you can estimate risks for future medical problems in a child by studying his placenta.

The mythic 'war' between the Æsir and the Vanir is the process of impregnation, pregnancy and also birth. There you go.

The Nine Worlds of Hel

There is a common misconception that Ásgarðr, Vanaheimr and other worlds too are names for the different nine worlds, but this is not true. The nine worlds are mentioned in Völuspá, but they are *not* named. So regardless of what some people claim about this, we simply don't know their names. In fact, from what we know, they don't have any names.

2.
Ek man jötna
ár of borna,
þá er forðum mik
fædda höfðu;
níu man ek heima,
níu íviðjur,
mjötvið mæran
fyr mold neðan.

2.

I remember ettins,
age old,
who fed me
ages ago,
nine worlds I remember,
nine in-woods,
famous destiny-tree
below the earth.

As I explained in 'Sorcery and Religion in Ancient Scandinavia', a divine home, a world does not need to be a geographical location, but can perfectly well be a time period. Like a month. Every month of the ancient Scandinavian calendar was named as one of the homes of the deities. There are 13 of them, each with 4 weeks, making up 364 days, and then we have New Year's Day in addition to that, which lasts for 2 days every leap year. And yes, this was not their only calendar. They also had a 12 month solar calendar and they used both.

Now, let us return to the second stanza of Völuspá. Knowing that a world can be a month will allow us to understand what the stanza tells us:

The child remembers nine worlds, that is *months*, in the womb of the mother, as it developed and grew (built nine in-woods) whilst hanging in the famous world tree, as described in 'Paganism Explained Part IV', in the womb (below the earth). These nine months can be any of the months of the calendar, as women don't all become pregnant at the same time, so you cannot name them in a myth.

This explains why age old ettins fed her. The placenta is a monster to the mother of the child, feeding on her, so that it can feed the child. Since it is also the sum of your forebears, it is indeed age-old.

The nine worlds are also mentioned in Vafþruðnismál:

43.

Frá jötna rúnum
ok allra goða
ek kann segja satt,
því at hvern hef ek
heim of komit;
níu kom ek heima
fyr niflhel neðan;
hinig deyja ór helju halir.

43.

From the secrets of the ettins
and all gods
I can tell,
because I have been
in all worlds;
in nine worlds I came,
below the hidden fog,
here comes the dead from the hidden halls.

Yes, he knows the secrets, because he has been educated for nine months in the womb of the mother, by Mímir, the placenta. It reminded him of all his previous lives.

As he is born, the dead come, the forebears, from the hidden halls. They are in him. They are him. He has become them. See 'Paganism Explained Part IV'.

No, the nine worlds are not named. They don't need to be.

Hel

Hel? You see no mention of it here. You want me to talk about Hel too, whilst we are on the subject of worlds in Scandinavian mythology? Okay, I will.

Hel derives from a PIE root *cel-/*kel-*, that means 'conceal' or 'hidden'. The term 'hall' too derives from this; it conceals/hides what is inside. Again we have a reference to the womb of the mother, a hidden world – from whence all the dead come. When they are re-born in you.

hinig deyja ór helju halir.
("here comes the dead from the hidden halls.")

After nine months, that is...

In 'Paganism Explained Part IV' I show you how Valhöll too is a name for the womb, and it is tempting to suggest that all references to 'hall' in the mythology is a reference to the womb of the mother.

Note that the burial mound is a symbolic womb of the mother, a symbolic Hel, and that when the dead are laid to rest there, they are because they are assumed to return to life. But only the honourable were buried that way. The men who had won good Hamingja in life.

Others were not buried like that, because they were not deemed worthy of a return to life, or at least they were not promoted to be chosen for rebirth like that. Some, those they deemed to be "degenerates", where according to Cornelius Tacitus in his 'Germania' instead executed and thrown into bogs, where "nothing" grows and where nothing can be easily recovered.

They wanted to get rid of them and also to make sure they never returned to life.

In this we see a type of natural morality. They had a strong desire to promote the honurable and remove the degenerate. The execution of the degenerate was not a punishment as such, but simply a way to do what is right; get rid of it.

And speaking of the mysterious Hel, we should continue on that track, and enter the mysterious realm of fairy tales. Let's explain a fairy tale here and now!

The Seventh Father in the House

Once upon a time a man was travelling. After long he came to a big and beautiful farm, with a mansion so magnificent it could well have been a small castle. "It will be nice to get some rest here", he said to himself when he had come inside the gate in the surrounding fence. Close by an old man with gray beard and hair was chopping wood.

"Good evening, father", the traveller said, "can I stay in your house tonight?"

"I am not the father in the house", the old man said, "go inside to the kitchen, and talk to my father!"

The traveller went inside to the kitchen, and there he met a man even older, sitting on his knees in front of the fire place, blowing on the heat (fire-place).

"Good evening, father, can I stay in your house tonight?" the traveller said.

"I am not the father in the house", the old man said, "go inside and talk to my father, he sits by the table in the living room!"

The traveller went to the living room and spoke to the man sitting at the table. He was much older than both the others, and he sat there, shivering and shaking, his teeth chattering, and was reading in a large book, almost like a little child.

"Good evening, father, can I stay in your house tonight?" the traveller said.

"I am not the father in the house", the old man said, "go and talk to my father, he sits inside the bench!" said the man who sat there, shivering

and shaking, with teeth chattering.

The traveller then went to the man who sat inside the bench, who was about to prepare tobacco for his pipe, but he was so huddled up and his hands shook so much that he had problems holding on to the pipe.

"Good evening, father", the traveller said again. "Can I stay in your house tonight?"

"I am not the father in the house", the old huddled up guy said, "go and talk to my father, he lies in the bed!"

The traveller went to the bed, and there he found an old, old man, whose only signs of life were a pair of big eyes.

"Good evening, father, can I stay in your house tonight?" the traveller said.

"I am not the father in the house", the old man with the big eyes said, "go and talk to my father, he lies in the crib!"

Yes, the traveller went to the crib, and there he found an exceedingly old man, so huddled up that he was no bigger than an infant, and he could not detect any life in him, other than some sounds coming from his throat every now and then.

"Good evening, father, can I stay in your house tonight?" the traveller said.

A long time passed before he received an answer, and even longer it took for him to finish his answer, but he said like the others, that he was not the father, "but talk to my father, he hangs in the horn on the wall."

The traveller stared up at the wall, and finally he spotted the horn, but when he looked at the man hanging in it, it was not much more to look at than a white spot resembling a human face.

He then became so afraid that he screamed out: "Good evening, father, can I stay in your house tonight?"

A squeeking sound much like that from a great titmouse could be heard, and he could barely tell that it was supposed to be the same as: "Yes, my child!"

And then a table with all the most precious dishes and with beer and booze came in, and when he had eaten and drinked, a good bed with raindeer calf skin came in, and the traveller was very happy that he after much time had found the right father in the house.

As you can already imagine, this is about reincarnation again. The seven fathers represent the first seven years of life, when we go through a dramatic change and end up in the age of reason. The traveller is a child of age seven finding back to himself.

The purpose of the reincarnation ritual is to recapitulate what has happened to you the first seven years of life. So the traveller arrives to see the youngest of the seven fathers, himself at age seven, cutting the umbilical cord outside the house, with an axe, and being reborn as one of his ancestors.

He then goes back in time and enters the house (womb) to find back to who he is and to be accepted as himself: as the reincarnated ancestor. The purpose is to become *aware* of himself and who he is.

He only realises who he is after talking to the seventh father, who tells him: "Yes, my child", instead of the normal "talk to my fahter." Only then does he become *aware* of himself and who he is.

The drinking horn on the wall is the 'holy grail', the placenta, giving blood to (feeding) the fetus in the womb. The seventh father is the traveller himself as a fetus and the ancestor in the placenta transferring the *Hamingja* to him.

The first seven years of life he doesn't know who he is, but when he goes through the reincarnation ritual this changes, and he becomes aware of who he is. He has been his ancestor all the time, but only now he knows. Only now he is aware of it. He is finally really reborn. Reincarnated.

Butter-Goat

Once upon a time a woman sat and baked. She had a small boy who was thick and fat, and who very much wanted good food, and therefore she called him Butter-Goat, and she had a dog called Golden-Tooth. Suddenly the dog started to bark.

"Run out, my Butter-Goat" the woman said, "and have a look at who Golden-Tooth barks at."

The boy ran out, came back in and said: "Oh dear god, a big and long burrow-woman is coming, carrying her own head under the arm and with a sack on her back."

"Run under the baking table and hide," *his mother told him.*

The the large troll entered.

"Good day!" *she said.*

"God bless!" *said Butter-Goat's mother.*

"Isn't Butter-Goat home today?" *the troll asked.*

"No, he is out in the forest hunting grouse with his father," *the mother replied.*

"What a troll that was, then!" *said the burrow-*

woman, "because I had such a nice little silver knife that I wanted to give him."

"Peep, peep! Here I am!" said Butter-Goat under the baking table.

"I am so old and my back is so stiff, " the troll said. "You should jump into my sack and pick it up yourself."

Once Butter-Goat had entered deep and well into the sack, the troll slung it on her back and went out the door. But after they had left a stretch behind them the troll got tired and asked: "How far is it to home?"

"Half a quarter (of a Norwegian mile)", Butter-Goat answered.

Then the troll put down the sack by the road and went through the copsewood on her own and lay down to sleep. In the meanwhile Butter-Goat saw his chance, took his knife, cut a hole in the sack and escaped. He placed a large pine root in the sack in his place, and hurried back to his mother. When the troll came home and saw what she had in her sack she became very angry.

The day after the women was baking again. Suddenly the dog started to bark.

"Run out, my Butter-Goat" the woman said, "and have a look at who Golden-Tooth barks at."

The boy ran out, came back in and said: "Oh no, oh no, that ugly beast!" Butter-Goat said. "She returns with her head under the arm and a big sack on her back."

"Run under the baking table and hide," his mother told him.

The the large troll entered.

"Good day!" she said, "is Butter-Goat home today?".

"No, he is out in the forest hunting grouse with his father," the mother replied.

"What a troll that was, then!" said the burrow-woman, "because I had such a nice little silver fork that I wanted to give him."

"Peep, peep! Here I am!" said Butter-Goat and came out from his hiding-place.

"I am so old and my back is so stiff, " the troll said. "You should jump into my sack and pick it up yourself."

Once Butter-Goat had entered deep and well into the sack, the troll slung it on her back and went out the door. But after they had left a *stretch behind them the troll got tired and asked: "How far is it to home?"*

"Half a (Norwegian) mile", Butter-Goat answered.

Then the troll put down the sack by the road and climbed up through the woods on her own and lay down to sleep. Whilst the troll did that Butter-Goat cut a hole in the sack and when he had escaped he placed a large rock in the sack. When the troll came home she kindled a fire in the fireplace and put a large cauldron on the fire and was about to boil Butter-Goat. But when she took the sack and was about to put Butter-Goat in the cauldron the rock fell out and knocked a hole in the cauldron, so that the water ran out and put the fire out. The troll became very angry and said: "Even if he makes himself as heavy as he can, I will trick him anyhow."

The third day it went the same way. Golden-Tooth barked and Butter-Goat's mother said: "

"Run out, my Butter-Goat" the woman said, "and have a look at who Golden-Tooth barks at."

The boy ran out, came back in and said: "Oh dear, the troll is back, carrying her own head under the arm and with a sack on her back."

"Run under the baking table and hide," his mother told him.

"Good day!" the troll said, and entered, "is Butter-Goat home today?"

"No, he is out in the forest hunting grouse with his father," the mother replied.

"What a troll that was, then!" said the burrow-woman, "because I had such a nice little silver spoon that I wanted to give him."

"Peep, peep! Here I am!" said Butter-Goat and emerged from under the baking-table.

"I am so old and my back is so stiff, " the troll said. "You should jump into my sack and pick it up yourself."

Once Butter-Goat had entered deep and well into the sack, the troll slung it on her back and went out the door. This time she didn't leave the sack alone and went to sleep, but instead went straight home with Butter-Goat in the sack. When they came home it was Sunday.

Then troll then said to her daughter: "Now you take Butter-Goat and butcher him and boil him and make a soup and have it ready until I return. I will go to church and ask others to join us for a feast."

When the troll had left the daughter was about to take Butter-Goat and butcher him, but she didn't really know hiw to.

"Wait, I will show you how to do that," Butter-Goat said. "Put your head on the stool, and you will see."

She did, poor her, and Butter-Goat took the axe and cut her head off as if she was a chicken. Then he puts the head in the bed and the rest of her corpse in the cauldron and made a soup. When he had done that he crawled up over the door and brought the pine root and the rock, and put one over the door and the other on the shelf above the fireplace.

When people came home from church and saw the head in the bed they thought that the daughter was sleeping, and they went over to the soup.

"Tastes good, Butter-Goat soup!" the woman said.

"Tastes good, daughter-soup!" said Butter-Goat. But they didn't listen.

The burrow-troll took the spoon and was about to taste.

"Tastes good, Butter-Goat soup!" he said.

"Tastes good, daughter-soup!" said Butter-Goat from the chimney above the fireplace.

They started to wonder, who was speaking, and wanted to go outside and have a look. But when they came out the door Butter-Goat threw the pine root and the rock on their heads and beat them to death. Then he took all the gold and silver in the house, and that made him very rich, and he travelled home to his mother.

At this point I am tempted to say: *Vituð ér enn eða hvat?* ("Do you still don't know enough or what?") You should be able to see the pattern by now, really. The tale is so clear and easy to interpret that I am tempted not to even explain anything.

Let us go through this together anyhow, though. If nothing else to make you understand that you were not wrong, and understood it correctly.

The woman who sat and baked is a pregnant woman. He small boy, who is thick and fat, is her baby in the womb. Therefore he loves good food. Babies greedily feeds on their mothers whilst in the womb, via the placenta.

Let us first explain why there is a dog called Golden-Tooth. At age seven you start to lose your milk teeth. You place the fallen tooth in a container, and the next day there is a piece of gold there instead. That is: as you age and the ancestor in you comes to the surface (the adult teeth), you become wiser ('wisdom is worth more than gold'). It's a dog in the fairy tales, because the dog (and wolf) is a metaphor for the reproductive organ of the woman. This is where you need to go to be reborn.

Notice also the fact that the dog is called by a name that we also know the deity Heimdalr as: *Gullintanni* ("Golden-Tooth"). He is by chance the guardian of the bridge leading to and from Ásgarðr.

When the dog starts to bark, it means that this is the moment the mother becomes pregnant.

The big and long burrow-woman is the foster mother, the She-Bear of the grave. Hence the description of her as big and long and a burrow-woman. The head she carries under her arm is Mímir, the placenta-ancestor.

The silver knife she brings is the key he needs to get out. It's one of the items he used to own in previous lives. It's there to help him remember and to reincarnate. It is a silver knife because it also shows us that he no longer breast feeds. He can eat real food. He has become seven years old.

She puts him in a sack, a metaphor for the womb, and carries him a distance. But she leaves him. She is the woman seeking solitude during birth, and he uses the key given to him to escape her womb. He leaves behind the placenta, the tree root, and is reborn. The first part of the reincarnation ritual has been completed.

He needs to go through three rebirths though. So the She-Bear returns, and the same happens again. The next time it's a silver fork, with the same function and purpose as the silver knife. The same happens again, only this time he leaves a rock in the sack. The rock is a petrified placenta.

When the burrow-woman returns home the rock knocks a hole in her cauldron and puts out the fire. Indeed, if the placenta becomes petrified the blood (fire) will stop running. This is a symbol of her placenta getting too old, signalling that it's time for the child to be born. Therefore it knocks a hole in her cauldron (womb). The second part of the reincarnation ritual has been completed.

I can add that a placenta will indeed turn to stone if it gets too old, it petrifies (yes, a pre-warning of a future Paganism Explained book about the Medusa....).

He needs to go through three rebirths though. Yes, like in all other fairy tales too. So the She-Bear returns, and the same happens again. The next time it's a silver spoon, with the same function and purpose as the silver knife and the silver fork.

This time she brings him home. Her home is another metaphor for the womb, and she brings him home to show us that he has gone further in the reincarnation ritual. It's a Sunday, because he is born on this day. He sees the Sun on the seventh day – at age seven.

In Scandinavia the week starts on the Monday, and ends on the Sunday. So yes, the Sunday is the seventh day of the week.

Her daughter is his twin. The burrow-woman is his mother, and if her daughter is in her womb (house) at the same time as Butter-Goat, she neccessarily has to be his twin sister. Like in other myths, the twin is always a metaphor for the placenta.

The mother tells her daughter to prepare the child for birth, which is of course what the placenta does, in the womb – during pregnancy. It feeds and prepares the child.

The church in this fairy tale is a modern addition, possibly added to make it possible to tell the fairy tale in Christian times, and it is a metaphor for the burial mound. Like in the church (with a grave yard), you will find sacred relics in the burial mound. The burrow... So the burrow-woman goes to collect the sacred object whom her forebears owned, to bring them home – to bring the memories of the forebears home, and thus bring them home. In the Stone Age this would have been a cave, and the burrow-woman a She-Bear. She enters the realm of death, to gather the dead. The feast she talks about is Butter-Goat's birth – and the re-birth of the forebears.

In every fairy tale with a child, the child is always very naive and ignorant in the beginning, and the troll is wise and smart. But with time, as Mímir (the placenta) transfers memories to the child the situation is reversed, and the child becomes wise and the troll stupid. Thus the daughter, his twin, the placenta, when he is about to be born, suddenly doesn't know anymore what to do. But he does. He tricks her into putting her head on the stool, to show her how to butcher him, and instead cuts her head off. He is born and the umbilical cord, connecting him to the placenta, is cut.

The detail "cut her head off as if she was a chicken" is not by chance, of course. This shows the bird as a metaphor for the womb with the placenta. The neck is the umbilical cord, and the wings the amniotic bag. Therefore many eat a bird (originally with a long neck) for dinner on the Yule eve (or you eat a pig, a metaphor for the same).

When the burrow-troll returns with the ancestors, Butter-Goat is still in the womb of the mother. The placenta is seemingly sleeping in the bed (the womb) and the soup is the amniotic fluid. This is the moment the child signals to the mother that it is ready to be born. He crawls up over the door and also the chimney. He places the pine root and the rock over the fireplace and the door, because both the pine root and the rock are metaphors for the placenta, and both the door and the fireplace with a chimney above it are metaphors for the vagina. This is where the child exits the womb.

The talk about the soup is the child communicating with the mother that it is ready to be born. When they go outside the door we see that all of a sudden Butter-Goat is in the chimney and above the door at the same time. Yes, because they are both the same thing. When he casts down the pine root and the rock, both symbols of the placenta, he is born. The mother no longer carries him, so her role as a bearer (a She-Bear) is terminated. The foster mother, the She-Bear, helping him reincarnate spiritually, likewise is no longer needed and her role is terminated. The ancestors are no longer in the placenta, but have been transferred to him. They are dead, but at the same time reborn in him. He has become them. They have become him. He has been given to himself. He has become his reincarnated forebears.

This is the reason why he can take all the gold and silver from the house. These are precious metals, in the case of gold non-corroding and eternal – just like the memories of the ancestors.

The third and final part of the reincarnation ritual has been completed and has made him spiritually rich, with the ancestors in him.

Sources for this book:

-*Samlagets Norrøn ordbok*, 5. utgåva, Oslo 2012

-Snorri Sturluson's *The Eddas.*

-Hjalmar Falk's, *Etymologisk Ordbog over det norske og det danske Sprog*, Kristiania 1906.

-Asbjørnsen og Moe's, *Eventyr*, J. M. Stenersens Forlag AS, Oslo 2009.

-Paternally expressed genes predominate in the placenta :
https://www.ncbi.nlm.nih.gov/pmc/articles/PMC3696791/

-Placental developmental defects in cloned mammalian animals :
https://www.ncbi.nlm.nih.gov/pubmed/27232488?log$=activity

-Altered Fetal Head Growth in Preeclampsia: A Retrospective Cohort Proof-Of-Concept Study :
https://www.ncbi.nlm.nih.gov/pmc/articles/PMC4595787/?log$=activity

-Placental Origins of Chronic Disease :
https://www.ncbi.nlm.nih.gov/pmc/articles/PMC5504455/?log$=activity

-Paternal age, placental weight and placental to birthweight ratio: a population-based study of 590,835 pregnancies :
https://www.ncbi.nlm.nih.gov/pubmed/23873147?log$=activity

-Gender differences in fetal growth and fetal-placental ratio in pre-eclamptic and normal pregnancies.
https://www.ncbi.nlm.nih.gov/pubmed/26105931

-The influence of head growth in fetal life, infancy, and childhood on intelligence at the ages of 4 and 8 years.
https://www.ncbi.nlm.nih.gov/pubmed/17015539

-The influence of birth size on intelligence in healthy children.
https://www.ncbi.nlm.nih.gov/pubmed/19482733

-Association of birthweight and head circumference at birth to cognitive performance in 9-10 year old children in South India: prospective birth cohort study
https://www.ncbi.nlm.nih.gov/pmc/articles/PMC3073480/

-Comparative placentation (in animals):
http://placentation.ucsd.edu/

-Placenta Abnormalities (in humans):
https://www.ncbi.nlm.nih.gov/books/NBK459355/

-Modeling the variability of shapes of a human placenta:
https://www.ncbi.nlm.nih.gov/pmc/articles/PMC2570048/

Other books by Varg Vikernes

-*Vargsmål*, Oslo 1997

-*Germansk Mytologi og Verdensanskuelse*, Stockholm 2000

-*Sorcery and Religion in Ancient Scandinavia*, London 2011

-*Reflections on European Mythology and Polytheism*, 2015

-*Mythic Fantasy Role-playing Game (MYFAROG)*, 2015

Other books by Marie Cachet

-*The Secret of the She-Bear* (originally written and also available in French as *Le secret de l'Ourse*, 2016)

-*Le besoin d'impossible*, 2009

Made in the USA
Las Vegas, NV
27 August 2024